How to Draw
Stuff
Real Easy

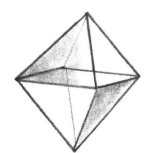

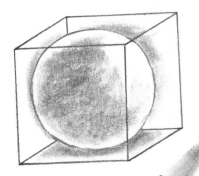

ShooRayner

For everyone who thinks they can't draw

This book is a revised and updated version of Shoo Rayner's popular book "Everyone Can Draw" by Shoo Rayner

Copyright © 2014/2022 Shoo Rayner

www.shoorayner.com

A Catalogue record for this book is available from the British Library

ISBN 978-1-908944-44-3

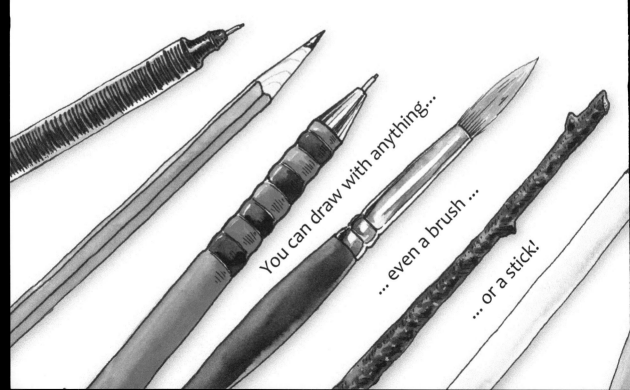

You can draw with anything...

... even a brush ...

... or a stick!

This is **NOT** a book about ART.
This is a book about **Drawing.**

You may not know it yet, but you are probably
quite good at drawing already!

With a few new drawing tricks, you will soon
be able to draw your own ideas with confidence.

Before you read this book, please sign your name below
and print your name underneath as neatly as you can.

PEN & PENCIL...

This book belongs to

Signature ....

Print Name ....

If you wrote your name on the previous page, then you can draw already! Writing is just one form of drawing.

You have probably spent years in school learning to draw the alphabet, so you are already a fantastic drawer.

First you learned how to make the marks that make letter shapes. Then you put the letters together to make words, then you put the words together to make sentences.

It's just the same with drawing. Marks go together to make shapes and the shapes go together to make drawings.

Look at the word, Box - it is made up from three different shapes - three lines, two semi-circles and a circle.

Look at a drawing of a box.
It is made from 9 lines
and 3 shades of blue.

The word "Box" and the drawing of a box mean the same thing. They are both "drawn" with marks that are "drawn" on the page.

The simplest mark you can make is a dot. The fun starts when you join two dots together with a line!

Here are two blue dots. Join them together with a line.

Well done - you can draw!

Drawing just means that you draw one object (maybe a pencil) across another object (maybe some paper) leaving a mark behind.

Some things are better for drawing with than others. Pencils are good. They are made to be easy to draw with. Paper is good. It is made to be drawn on.

You can draw with anything on any surface you can imagine: Felt-tip pen on a broken leg - pencil on wood - a stick in the sand. It's all drawing and the more you draw, the better you get.

All you will need with this book is a pencil and some paper. You might like to get a sketchbook or a pad, so you can keep all your drawing practice together in one place.

This is a great idea, because you can see how much your drawing has improved from one page to the next.

About Pencils

Pencil leads are not made of lead. Lead is a metal.
Pencil leads are made from Graphite, which is a type of carbon, which is what diamonds are made of too! But Diamonds are hard and shiny, while graphite is dull and soft.

Graphite is mixed with clay, to make it stick together, and with wax or oils, to make it draw smoothly over the page.

More clay makes the pencil lead hard. Less clay, or more wax and graphite, make the lead softer and darker.

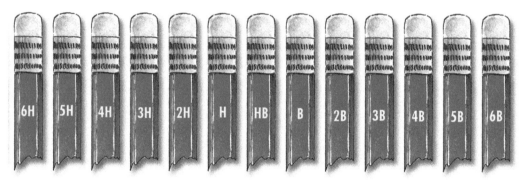

Pencils are marked H or B.
H means (H)ard and B means (B)lack.

6H is a very hard pencil. 6B is a very soft, dark pencil.

In the middle is HB. This is the everyday kind of pencil that is used in schools and offices.

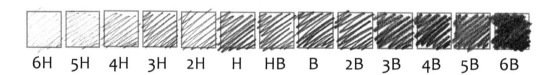

Different grades of pencil give different shades of grey.

Keep your pencil sharp and hold the pencil vertically to the paper to draw fine lines.

(Don't forget the pencil sharpener!)

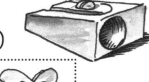

Tip: You can buy spare blades for pencil sharpeners that have gone blunt.

Lean the pencil at a shallow angle to the paper and use the side edge of the graphite to draw wide lines.

This is good for shading and can be used for some great effects. Try it and see!

Mechanical pencils have fine leads that don't need sharpening. The graphite is mixed with high polymer plastic to make the leads really strong.

Mechanical pencils come in different lead thickness sizes and can be filled with soft or hard leads. They are great for technical drawing.

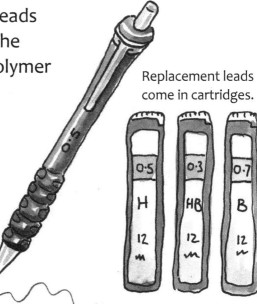

Replacement leads come in cartridges.

Practice

Whatever you want to be good at, you need to practice.

Whether you want to be a musician, a gymnast, a soccer player or a hairdresser, you need to practice to become really good at your chosen field of endeavour.

If you want to improve and be really good at drawing you need to practice too. If you love drawing, it will be a pleasure to look forward to - you won't even think of it as practice.

Make it easy! Get a sketchbook or a pad and keep it close to hand so you can draw without having to go and find paper and pencil every time you want to draw.

Drawing in a sketchbook is like writing a diary. It's private, so you can make lots of mistakes without worrying what people will say. You can also see how much you improve.

Try and draw something everyday, it doesn't matter what. Draw even if you only have two minutes to spare.

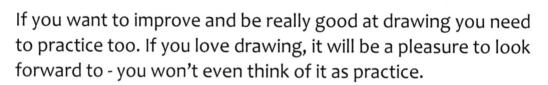

2D or 3D?

We live in a three dimensional world of Length, Height and Depth.
The surface of a sheet of paper only has two dimensions –
width and height.

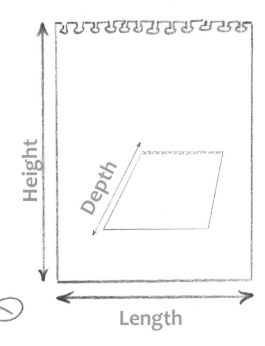

A 2D, or Two Dimensional drawing looks flat.

We create the illusion of 3D, or Three Dimensions, by adding another line that appears to go backward to create Depth.
Really it is just going at a different angle to the height and depth. Shading makes drawings look even more real.

When you see a drawing that looks "real", or like a photograph, it is a 3D Representation of an image on a 2D surface.

Triangles and Prisms

Remember how you drew a line between two points? Now, add a third point. A Triangle is created when all the points are connected.

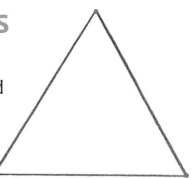

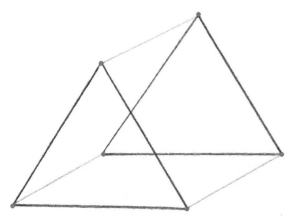

Draw another triangle with one of the points in the middle of the first triangle and connect the corresponding corners with lines. You have made a Wire-Frame drawing of a Prism.

It is easy to draw a prism from any angle - from above, below or from the side.

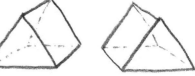

You might recognise this shape in a famous chocolate bar or the tent you might sleep in if you go camping.

Squares and Boxes

Connecting four points together creates a **Rectangle**.

In this case it is a **Square**.

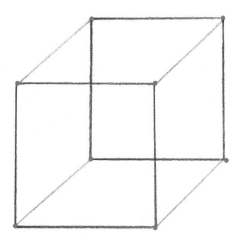

Draw two squares. Put the corner of one square in the middle of the other square. Connect up the corresponding corners and you have made a wire-frame drawing of a **Cube** or **Box**.

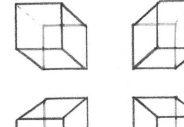

Again, it is easy to draw the box from any angle - from above, below or from the side.

We can use the cube shape to draw dice, blocks and Rubik's Cubes.

See the videos at
www.shoorayner.com/courses

Rectangles and Boxes

Changing the width or the height of the square, will create a rectangle. Draw two identical rectangles and connect up the four corners, just like the cube. This creates a wire-frame drawing of a Rectangular Box.

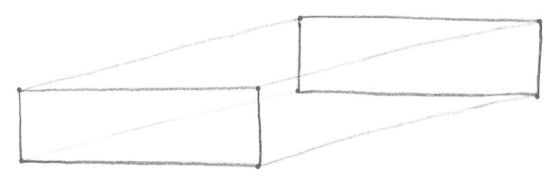

There are so many things you can draw with boxes. It's good to practice to draw these shapes a lot.

A Tile is just a very thin box!

Circles and Cylinders and Disks

Circles work exactly the same way as triangles and rectangles.

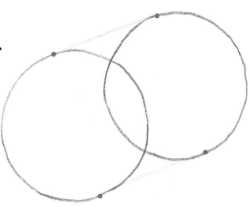

Draw two circles and connect up the top and bottom edges. By doing this you will make a wire-frame drawing of a Cylinder.

Rearrange the circles to change the length of the cylinder and angle that you view bit from.

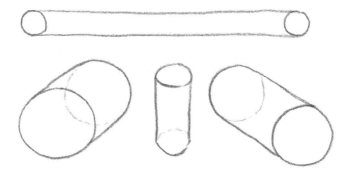

You can also join the circles together with curved lines to make interesting and curly-whirly shapes!

A Disk is just a very thin cylinder!

13

Circles, Cylinders and Tubes

A Tube is a cylinder with a hole through the middle of its length.

Draw a cylinder by connecting up two circles. Draw smaller circles inside the first circles and join them up too. Depending of the shape and angle of the tube, you may not see the opening circle at the back of the tube.

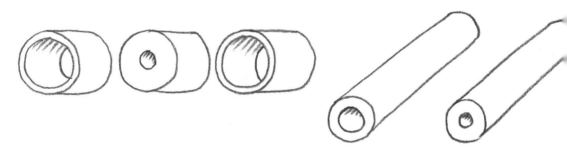

Tubes can be long and thin, like hose pipes, short like pasta curved, like macaroni or quite flat, like sticky tape or chunky like toilet rolls.

Ellipses

Ellipses are squashed circles. To understand what an ellipse is, draw a square with a circle fitting neatly inside it.

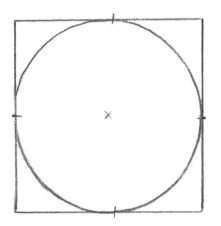

The circle will just touch the four sides of the square in the middle of each edge.

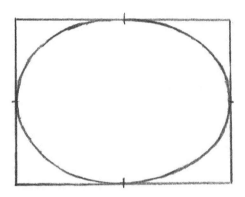

Now draw a rectangle and draw a squashed circle inside it, so it just touches the edges of the rectangle at the centre point of each edge.

You have drawn an ellipse!

Draw a 3D cube and fit circles and ellipses inside the top, facing and side surface. Make the circles and ellipses touch at the centre point of each edge.

These ellipses represent 3D circles and add to the 3D effect.

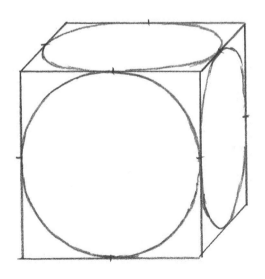

See the videos at
www.shoorayner.com/courses

Different Shapes

Parallelograms have two pairs of parallel sides

The previous drawing was made from a square with a circle inside and two leaned-over rectangles, or **Parallelograms**, each with an ellipse inside them.

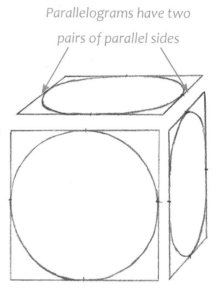

We can do similar things with these and other shapes as we did with triangles rectangles and circles.

Building up your drawings with ellipses and rectangles make cylinders and boxes look even more 3D.

Try drawing 3d shapes built up from other 2D shapes

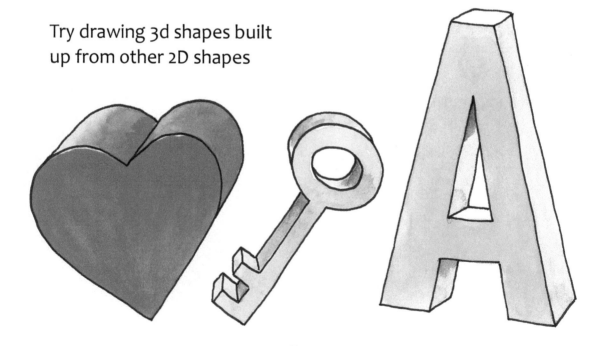

Cones and Pyramids

Draw an ellipse and place a single point above it.

Draw lines from the edges of the ellipse to the point to make a wire frame drawing of a Cone.

Draw a parallelogram with a single point above it.

Connect the corners of the parallelogram to the point to make a wire-frame drawing of a Pyramid.

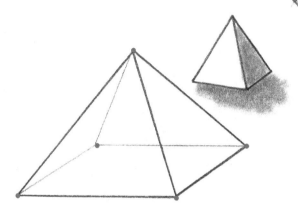

Put two pyramids together and you will make a wire-frame drawing of a Diamond.

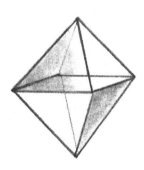

Draw any shape and connect the corners to a point above the shape and you will make wire-frame shapes like mountains, pyramids and stars.

Spheres

Imagine holding a circular loop of wire at the top and the bottom.

When you spin it round fast, the wire will make a **Ball** shape or **Sphere**.

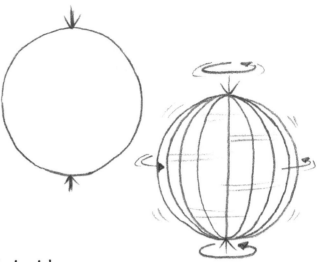

Just as a circle fits perfectly inside a square, a sphere fits perfectly inside a cube

The sphere touches the exact centre of every face of the cube.

We can find the centre of a square by joining the opposite corners. The point where the lines cross will be the centre of the square.

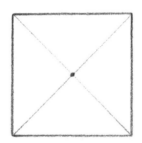 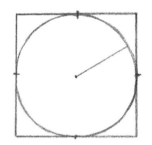

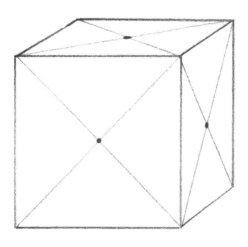

It is the same for a cube. We can find the centre of each face of a cube by joining the opposite corners of each face. The point where they cross marks the centres of each face.

Using those points we can draw ellipses to show how the sphere fits inside the cube.

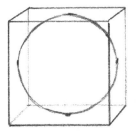 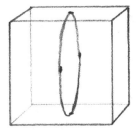 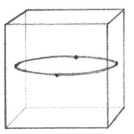 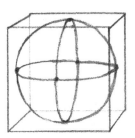

Draw a circle all the way around the shapes of the ellipses and you will have a 3D representation of a sphere.

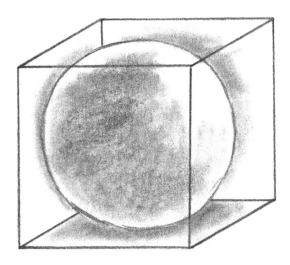

Another way to understand spheres is to imagine them like a globe, or a model of the Earth, which is crisscrossed with lines of Longitude and Latitude.

Practice this exercise a lot, so you can draw the sphere from any angle.

See the videos at
www.shoorayner.com/courses

19

Putting 3D Shapes Together

Most of the things you are ever likely to draw are made up from boxes, circles, cones, cylinders, tubes and spheres. Try drawing these easy examples.

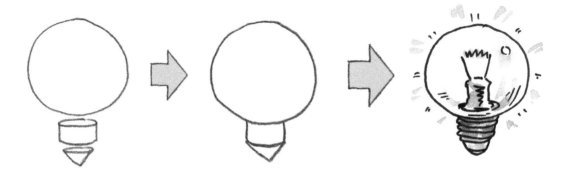

Draw the light bulb for the lamp stand.

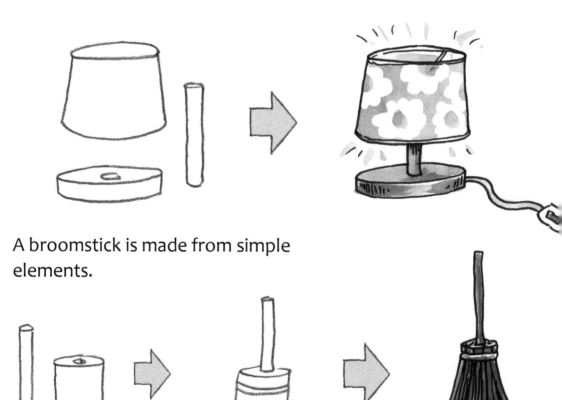

A broomstick is made from simple elements.

A snowman is really just a few circles, one on top of an other.

That's what the broomstick is for!

A circle and a stick make a lollipop or a tree.

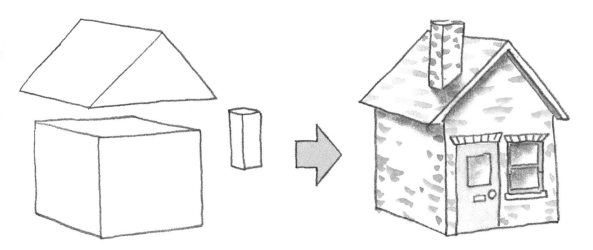

Two boxes and a prism make a house.

Perspective

Perspective is how we trick the eye into thinking there is depth in a 2D picture. One way you might find it easier to understand is to imagine playing with building blocks on a base board.

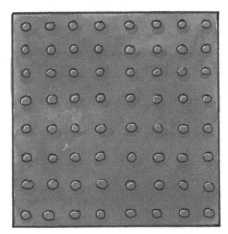

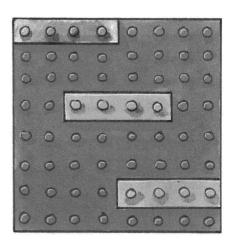

Top view

From above, the blocks all look the same shape. Viewed from the side and above, the blocks at the front appear larger than the blocks at the back. Try measuring them to be sure!

Side and above view

We can make things even simpler by drawing a square and splitting it up into 16 smaller squares.

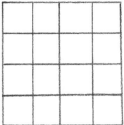

When the square is squashed down into a parallelogram it looks like the square is a sheet lying on the ground. This gives a 3D effect of depth.

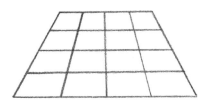

If we continue drawing the lines upward, they will eventually cross each other. Where the lines meet is called the Vanishing Point.
The horizontal line where they all meet is called the Horizon.

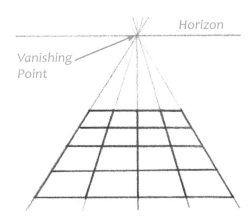

This is called One Point Perspective. All the lines that give the impression of depth meet at the same point on the horizon.

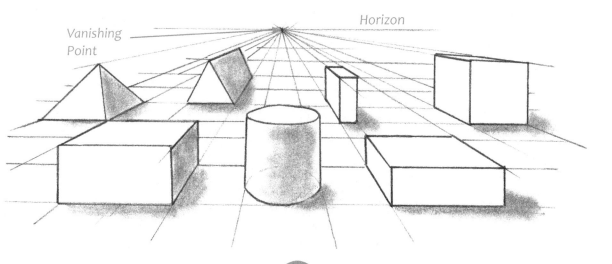

Two Point Perspective

One point perspective is a great and simple effect.

Drawings can be made to look even more realistic. **Two Point Perspective** works the same way as one point, but this time we have two vanishing points on the horizon line.

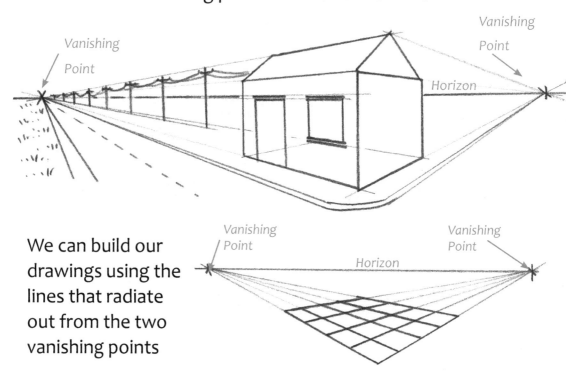

We can build our drawings using the lines that radiate out from the two vanishing points

This makes a more satisfying and interesting impression of 3D.

By creating a wire frame box, we can make a wire-frame room and fill it with furniture. This simple way of planning will make your drawings look more real.

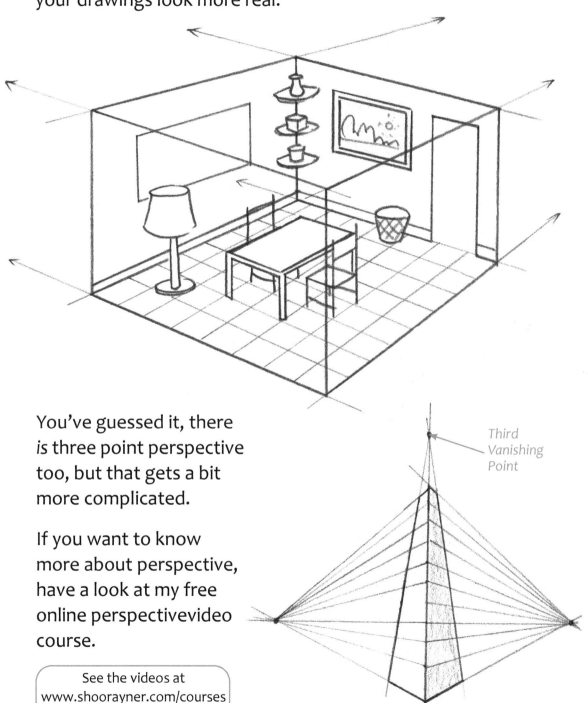

You've guessed it, there *is* three point perspective too, but that gets a bit more complicated.

If you want to know more about perspective, have a look at my free online perspectivevideo course.

Third
Vanishing
Point

See the videos at
www.shoorayner.com/courses

Light and Shade

The other way to trick the eye into thinking a 2D drawing is really 3D, is to use Shading.

Let's go to hot, sunny Egypt and look at how the sun creates Shadows on the pyramids.

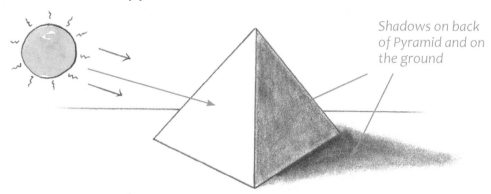

Shadows on back of Pyramid and on the ground

As the sun arcs across the sky through the day, the angle at which the light falls on the pyramids changes.

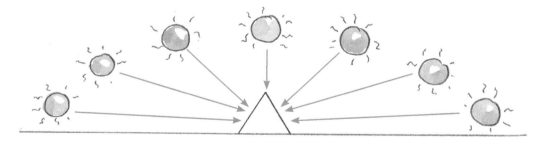

The angle of the light from the sun changes through the day, making the shadows on the pyramid move and change too.

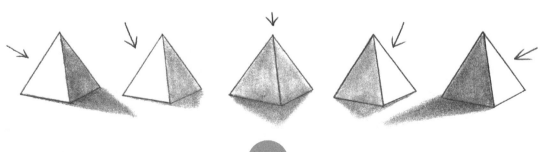

Light and shade is a little more complicated than just having the sunlight pouring down in one direction. The sky and the sand are bright and reflect light.

The sky gives a soft, **Ambient** glow and the sand also **Reflects** sunlight back onto the pyramids.

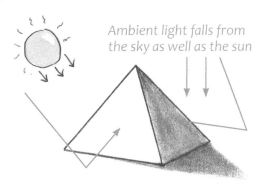

Ambient light falls from the sky as well as the sun

Imagine a sphere lying on the sand in the desert in Egypt.

The shadow of the sphere is cast on the ground.
The sphere itself is shaded where the sun doesn't reach.
But light is reflected up from the sand, so the back edge of the sphere is illuminated gently too. All this adds up to create a really satisfying 3D effect.

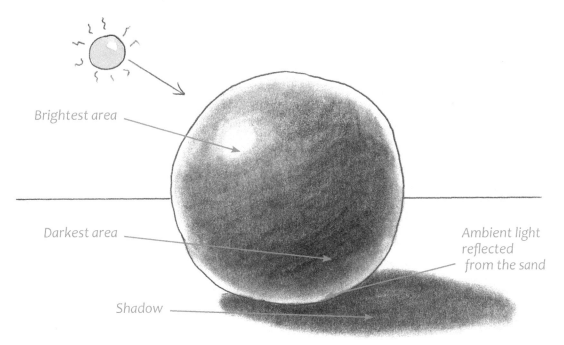

Brightest area

Darkest area

Ambient light reflected from the sand

Shadow

Shading

There are several ways to create shading effects. One way is to Shade in Pencil. When you press hard on the pencil the shading will be dark. When you press lightly the shading will be light.

Practice shading exercises. Begin by pressing hard with your pencil. As you move across the page, press more and more lightly until the pencil is no longer touching the paper.

This is called Graduated Shading.

When you shade a sphere, there will be a crescent moon-shaped area of darkness furthest away from the light source, and a light area where the light is strongest.

Try to practice this a lot.

Brightest area

Darkest area

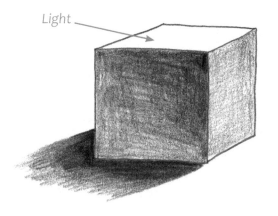

Light

When you shade a box, the side of the box in the light will be the lightest and the side furthest away will be darkest. There may be some reflected light, so the darkest side might be lighter at the bottom of the face.

Cross-Hatching and Stippling

There are many other methods of shading.

Cross-Hatching builds shade by overlaying lines at different angles while shortening the strokes. This works really well with ink but is also good with pencil.

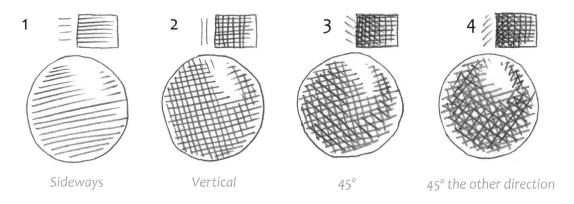

1 Sideways 2 Vertical 3 45° 4 45° the other direction

Stippling works best in ink. The shade is built up by drawing hundreds of dots. This might drive you dotty, but it is a really good effect if you take time and care!

All in a Spin

For some shapes, it is best to imagine them being made by a woodworker, cutting away the wood as it spins round very fast on a lathe. Or by a potter, raising the shape of a vase as the clay spins round on the potter's wheel.

The Inuit people of Arctic used to say that a walrus tusk, or a whale's tooth, contains a carving inside it already.
All you have to do is take away the surface to reveal the sculpture inside. If you want to draw a vase, imagine it being carved out of a block - imagine that the vase is already inside.

Many objects are made this way. If you can draw a box or a cylinder from any angle, you will be able to draw the cup or space rocket or candle stick that is "carved out" of your shape at any angle too.

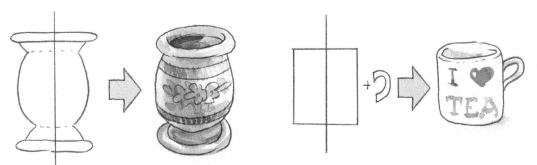

The outline of the sideways view is called the Profile. The vase is a cylinder with bumpy bits while the mug is a cylinder with a handle.

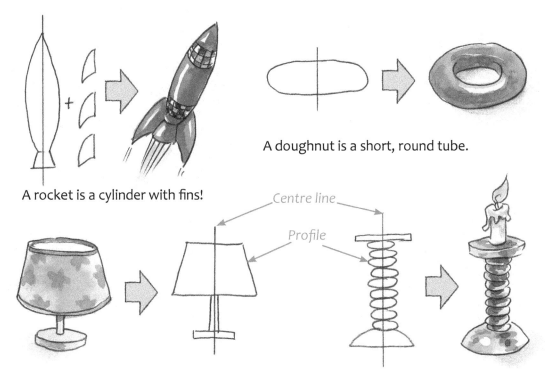

A doughnut is a short, round tube.

A rocket is a cylinder with fins!

These shapes are made by Spinning a profile around a centre line.

Draw People

One of the things we want to draw most is people.

If you can draw Stick Men, you are half way to doing great drawings of people. Stick men drawings are a great way of getting the pose you want very quickly.

Try doing lots of these quick sketches to get the feel of how the body moves. Work from photographs or ask your friends to pose for you in different and silly positions!

All you have to do is draw the pose you want and put clothes on your stick man model - and a face... and hair... and shoes... and hands... So much to learn! Never mind, practice and build up your skills slowly.

Draw your people with stick men as the central core of the figure, then build the body around the core. (Remember, if you draw in ink, you can erase the pencil lines afterwards!)

It may look simple, but most great artists start with simple stick men sketches.

Draw Heads

Now you know why you spent so long learning how to draw spheres! A head is basically a sphere.

Remember how we drew spheres back on page 18? A cross drawn on the front will look different as the sphere is moved round. The lines of the cross curve as the sphere Rotates.

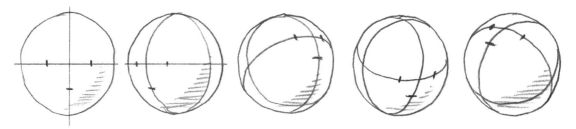

Add eyes, nose, mouth and ears – how about some hair?

Add a chin on the bottom to make the character look older. Now the sphere has turned into a sort of egg shape, but we can make it face in different directions just the same.

The brain box of a human skull is like a sphere.
The face is like a shield stuck on the front.

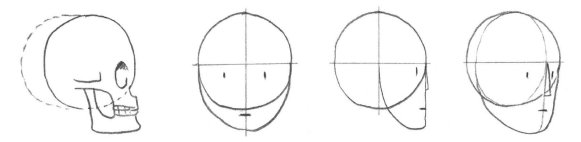

Try experimenting with different types of body. Babies have huge heads and squashed up bodies. Children's heads are quite big compared to the rest of their body.

An adult's head might not be much bigger than that of a child but their body will be much bigger.

See the videos at
www.shoorayner.com/courses

Draw Hair

Most people don't draw enough hair. When you think you are finished draw some more!

Look at magazines to find ideas for hairstyles. Ask friends to pose for you and draw their hair, then you can see how the hair falls at the back. Try drawing hair from many angles.

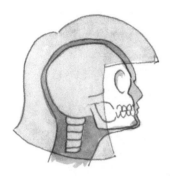

Hair is usually much bigger than the head underneath it.

Some people have no hair and some people have lots!

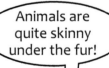

Don't worry too much about individual hairs!
Just draw the overall shape.

Animals are quite skinny under the fur!

Draw Hands and Feet

When drawing hands, think of the palm as a circle. The four fingers stick out roughly at 90° to the thumb. Plan the drawing very lightly and then draw darker around the outside.

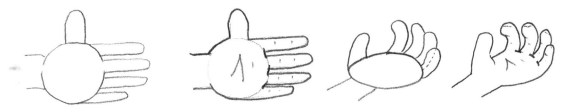

For a more 3D effect, do the same, but imagine the circle is a disk and the fingers are cylinders, or sausages!

The sole of the foot is a sort of ellipse. Connect the ellipse to the leg, as if you are connecting a cone to a cylinder.

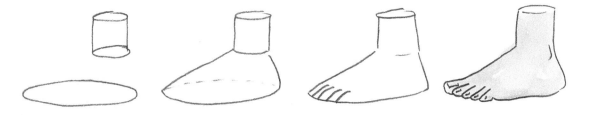

Make the sole thicker, like a disk, and draw a shoe the same way.

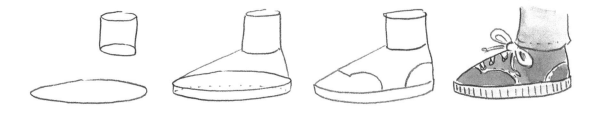

Drawing More Realistic Poses

You might like to get a wooden model mannequins to help you draw poses. When you draw them from the front, they are made up from very simple 2D shapes. Change those 2D shapes into their 3D equivalents.

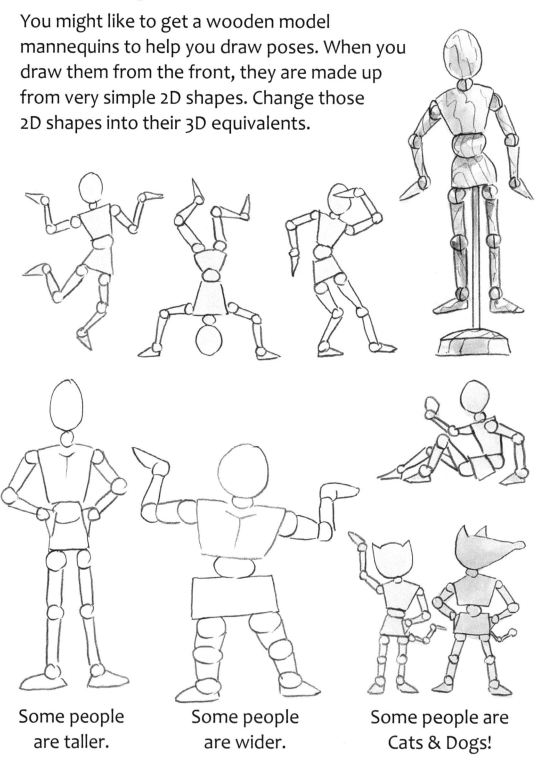

Some people are taller.

Some people are wider.

Some people are Cats & Dogs!

If you've been practicing, you know how to make those 2D shapes look 3D. Draw lots of these models and you will soon understand how to draw people in all sorts of poses.

Then all you need to do is put clothes on the body.

Draw Faces

Get yourself a mirror! You know the expression you are after so be your own model. A three-way dressing table mirror is even better!

The easiest eyes to draw are just circles with dots inside them. The characters can look in any direction or at each other.

Most of the eyeball is hidden behind the eyelids. The colourful **Iris** is often half-hidden under the eyelids. Showing the whole of the iris makes the character stare or look a little crazy!

A white blob in the **Pupil** represents the **Highlight Reflection** that makes the eye "look alive!"

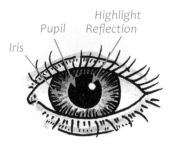

Normal   Staring

The simplest eyes are just dots.
Noses can be all sorts of weird and wonderful shapes.

Eyes, mouths and eyebrows change the Expression of a face. Learn all the different combinations to build up a vocabulary of feelings and emotions that bring your drawings alive.

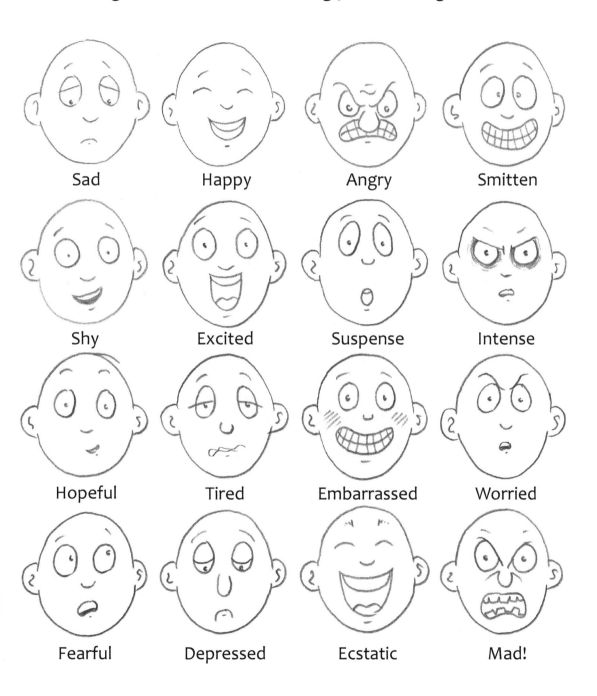

| Sad | Happy | Angry | Smitten |

| Shy | Excited | Suspense | Intense |

| Hopeful | Tired | Embarrassed | Worried |

| Fearful | Depressed | Ecstatic | Mad! |

Draw Animals

Animals have skeletons just like humans. Try to imagine them as models under the fur and feathers. Their bones are not always where you think they are!

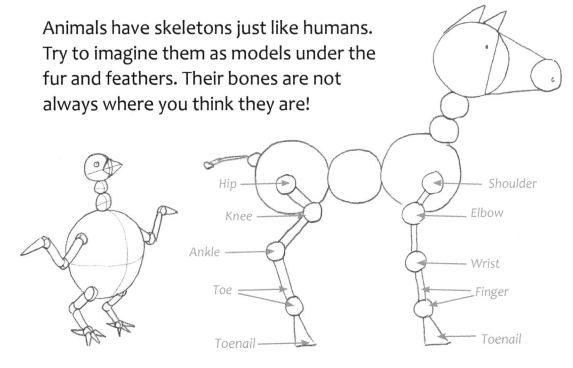

First understand the animal in 2D shapes and outlines.

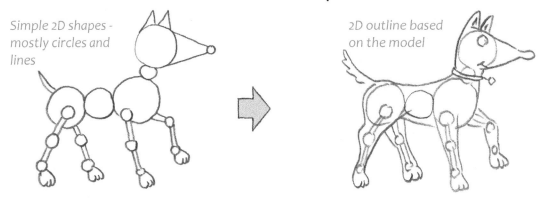

Simple 2D shapes - mostly circles and lines

2D outline based on the model

Turn 2d into 3D shapes that you can draw from any angle.

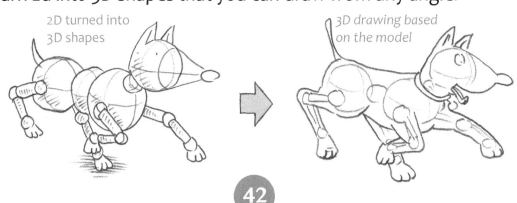

2D turned into 3D shapes

3D drawing based on the model

Animals can be drawn using the simplest shapes.

Don't look at the animal! Always look at the basic shapes
that make up the shape you are trying to draw.

Draw Stuff

Now you can draw just about anything. Use all the basic shapes you have learned and practiced throughout this book.

The more you draw, the more you will see the shapes in the things you draw, so try and draw something every day.
That is how you will slowly get better and better.

Swans and skulls are mostly curves and circles

Minecraft characters are all made from boxes

This heart and the guitar body are both rounded box shapes

HEART OF STONE

See the videos at
www.shoorayner.com/courses

A skateboard is made from disks and cylinders

Dice are just boxes

A tea pot is a ball with a hole in the top and a hole in the side!

Drink cans are basically cylinders

Phones and padlocks are boxes with shaped corners and edges.

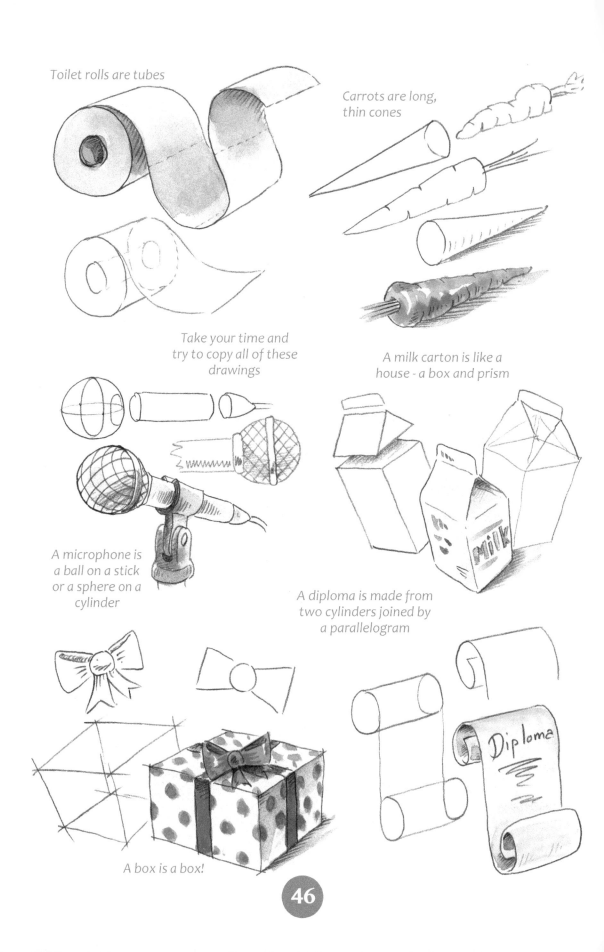

Toilet rolls are tubes

Carrots are long, thin cones

Take your time and try to copy all of these drawings

A milk carton is like a house - a box and prism

A microphone is a ball on a stick or a sphere on a cylinder

A diploma is made from two cylinders joined by a parallelogram

A box is a box!

A gravestone is a box with half a disk on top

An ice cream cone gets its name because it is a cone!

A muffin is a flared tube or section of a cone with a blob on the top!

Both the hotdog roll and the sausage are spheres cut in half with a cylinder placed in between the two halves

A computer mouse is basically a sphere cut in half

A jet airliner is a tube with wings!

Get a sketchbook

Keeping a sketchbook is like having an artist's studio in your pocket.

Sketch while you wait.

Keep a sketchbook and pencil handy and you can start drawing straight away without having to get stuff out of drawers or cupboards. And you don't have to tidy away.

No one *Sketch stuff!* ever has to look in your sketchbook, so you can make millions of mistakes and make it as messy- and private - as you like!

Small sketchbooks fit in a pocket so you can draw anywhere, anytime. Larger sketchbooks are great for practicing and working out your ideas.

Sketch friends.

The more you sketch the better you will draw and the more confident

you will become. Your sketchbooks will add up to a mountain of ideas and experience, revealing just how much you are learning and improving.

Draw when you watch TV

Final advice

Practice is the absolute key to improving your drawing skills.

Draw a little bit every day to form a drawing habit.
Five minutes is enough to do a quick sketch during a lunch break or while waiting. It doesn't have to be a masterpiece! Just get your brain and hands used to the idea of drawing.

Break everything down into simple shapes, then practice drawing the shapes from different angles.

Soon you will find you are able to draw the ideas in your imagination. That's when the fun really begins – whole new worlds are waiting to be drawn from inside your head!

Keep working at it and visit my website to keep up to date with the free videos and drawing advice I give every week on YouTube.

Above all, enjoy yourself. Don't be too critical with yourself. Drawing is hard work, but it is a fantastic skill that builds self-confidence. Soon you will amaze yourself and your friends with your new-found skills.

Good Luck
& see you soon!

www.shoorayner.com